From Rags to Riches

Inspiring Stories of Ordinary People with Extraordinary Lives!

SAM WALTON

JOHN D ROCKEFELLER

I0435624

URSULA BURNS

ROSALIA MERA

SYLVESTER STALLONE

AND MORE

By Elda Watulo

Mendon Cottage Books

JD-Biz Corp Publishing

Copyright

TABLE OF CONTENTS

INTRODUCTION

Just like we need food for our body, our spirit also needs food that comes as motivating and touching stories, they can make us feel better and give us power to scale the financial heights. This book contains a collection of the most inspiring rags to riches stories. You will not only enjoy reading them but you will be motivated to move to a higher point in your financial world. Each story in this book comes with an important life changing lesson.

Rags-to-riches stories in this book have been told to inspire other people to rise from poverty and become rich. Most of the people in this book rose from obscurity to gain fame through many hurdles. Classic stories like the tales of Alladin and Cinderella are often treated as cases of such stories. The life of Gengis Khan who lived with his mother and siblings used to be homeless before he annexed lands which later became the largest empire. During the Roman Empire, the Emperor Diocletian was born poor to a slave father. Sir Gareth in the King Arthur story was a kitchen boy before he became a knight. In India, the Mauryan Emperor Chandragupta Maurya was also poor. In China, Emperor Gaozu and Hongwu Emperor came from a peasant class.

It is not easy to rise from poverty to a life of fame and fortune. A lot of stories had been written to inspire people to move out of their comfort zones to a life of immense wealth. Lessons from rags-to-riches stories have been published for readers to learn and apply them in their own lives.

HOW TO GET MOTIVATION AND INSPIRATION FOR SUCCESS

Why not believe in yourself in you can believe in something? The following are tips that will help you achieve your dreams and goals by changing your attitude and get inspired.

Be Sociable: People who have risen from poverty to wealth are known conversationalists. They know how to talk to people as well as subtly encourage these people to agree with them. They also show genuine interest to other people so it is easy for them to connect with them.

Learn the Value of Sacrifices: Successful people know how to make sacrifices. They have a vision. They make a lot of sacrifices to make that vision a reality.

Create a Brand: People who came out of poverty know not only of corporate branding but of personal branding as well. They live a life consistent to their own personal brand. They strive hard to inspire people with their life anecdotes. For these successful people, they are a priceless commodity. They are the complete package.

Be in the Company of People with the Same Vision: If you want to succeed hang out with people with the same goal because it is easy to imbibe the lackluster attitude of uninteresting, dull, and unambitious friends.

Catch the Sunrise: Successful people are often those people who wake up early. They do what they can do in the morning so that they have time for socializing and other personal needs at the end of the day. Successful people are those people who are always one day closer to their goal.

Exert the Best Effort in Every Task: Not everyone can multitask. Brainpower and focus are often compromised by people who strive to finish everything all at once. Successful people do their best in every task at hand so that they don't have to repeat it because the outcome turned out bad.

Be Generous: Generous people are often successful people. They selflessly give their time and resources to everyone in need. Thus, fate rewards them with success.

Live Life like A Game of Chess: A skillful chess player calculates his moves ahead. Every move must be towards one goal only: to win. People who want to succeed in life must plan their life accordingly. Focus is important if a person has the will to succeed.

Learn to Take Risks: Successful people are risk takers. Although it's good to have a back-up plan, they often work harder towards their goal if they know they don't have a back-up plan. Successful people are determined people. They are motivated to try their very best when no safety net will catch them if they fall.

Deliver Even the Smallest Promises: Successful people know how to keep their word. Trust for them is important. Thus, they stake everything to keep their promises.

Remain Humble: Humility is like a secret weapon for successful people. By being down-to-earth and charming, successful people are helped by a lot of people because they remain nice.

Don't give in to Fear: Fear holds back quite a number of people. These people are very much afraid to fail so they tend to procrastinate. Although a lot of people are afraid to commit mistakes, they must try to understand that mistakes are part and parcel of success. No one can avoid mistakes. Playing safe and not getting out of one's comfort zone are sure ways to remain stagnant in life. People who have big goals and big dreams must be ready to commit big mistakes. They may fail quite a number of times but they mustn't give up.

Remain Consistent: Success comes to those people who consistently strive to realize their dreams. They try to change their bad habits and develop good ones which can help them in making their visions come true. Acquiring a good attitude, habit, or skill will be a great help in the lives of people who try their best to be successful.

Stay Original: Successful people are trail blazers. They don't follow the bandwagon. They look for other ways to do things with the purpose of innovation. Most people are lazy by nature. People who want to succeed know where they want to go and how to get there. Discipline is important as well.

Be results oriented: Successful people are after the outcome. They know what they want to get out of every endeavor. It is easy for them to devise ways to reach the end because they know what the end is.

Strive for Long Term Happiness: Successful people don't like short cuts. They're not willing to settle. They accept the challenges now because they know they will be rewarded in the future. It may be stressful. It may hurt. However, people who want to be successful embrace every hardship because they believe there's happiness when they've accomplished their goals.

Be a Cut above the Rest: Successful people have a little extra when compared with other people. They are more patient in life. They know that taking consistent small steps can result to big changes in their lives. They create amazing results because they work extra hard for it.

Have an Action Plan: Successful people tend to make things happen because they are prepared to make them happen. They strive to be smarter by taking time to study or read. They do away with unnecessary things to have time to read. They are also more productive. Every day is a busy day for successful people. They try to fit what's important to them in their busy schedule. They don't mind waking up early so they can do things that need to be done. Successful people take care of their health. They do realize that they can't accomplish what they want to do if they're unhealthy. Thus, they keep a healthy lifestyle.

This e-book shares some of the best rags-to-richest stories of successful people. In each story, the reader is expected to learn a few valuable lessons which he can apply in his own life. The stories are meant to serve as an inspiration to everyone. Success is possible. Everyone has a chance at success. Poverty shouldn't be a hindrance in realizing one's dreams and aspirations. Everyone has a shot at getting rich. The road to financial success isn't easy but it is achievable. A lot of people have done it. There's no reason why you can't be like them.

MOTIVATING RAGS TO RICHES STORIES

SAM WALTON

The Man behind the Success of Wal-Mart

In the words of Sam Walton, the customer is the boss. He can fire everyone by buying somewhere else. Sam Walton is known as the man behind the world's largest retailer, Wal-Mart. He was able to transform every American's way of shopping and made himself a huge fortune in the process. He built his retail empire by targeting rural Americans.

The Early Life of Sam Walton

Samuel Moore Walton was born on March 29, 1918 in Kingfisher, Oklahoma, where his family owned a farm until 1923. After realizing that the farm was not earning enough profit to sustain a family, Sam's father, Thomas Walton, decided to resume his duties as a Farm Loan Appraiser. Thereafter, they would move from Oklahoma to Chesterfield, Missouri. In Missouri they would move from town to town, including Shelbina, where Sam became Missouri's youngest Eagle Scout while in the 8th grade.

His family eventually settled in Columbia, Missouri where he grew up during the Great Depression. Like many young people during that period, Sam Walton had to help the family in order to make ends meet. He milked the cow and delivered the bottled milk to customers. He also became a newspaper delivery boy while selling magazine subscriptions. When he graduated from high school at the David H. Hickman High School, he was awarded "Most Versatile Boy". Sam played football and basketball and was an honor student who served as the Class President of his senior class.

After high school, he attended the University of Missouri. He didn't come from a wealthy family, he joined the ROTC and also worked several jobs to feed and support himself. He joined The Zeta Phi Chapter of Beta Theta Pi and was also invited by the QEBH, a popular campus secret society (for honor students) within the university. He was also tapped by Scabbard and Blade, a national military honor society. He graduated with a degree in Economics in 1940. Not bad for a poor kid from humble beginnings.

Sam Walton's Life before Wal-Mart

In 1940, Sam Walton started with JC Penny in Des Moines, Iowa as a sales trainee, three days after he graduated. His boss almost fired him because of his failure to complete required paperwork. The reason for not completing the paperwork made total sense to him; he didn't want his customers to wait. Thus, he wasn't able to keep his books in order. Nevertheless, he earned $25 commissions monthly for his ability to sell his products.

In 1942, he was drafted by the United States Army and worked as a communications officer during World War II for the Army Intelligence Corps. In 1945, after leaving the military, he borrowed $20,000 from his father-in-law and together with his $5,000 he bought a Ben Franklin variety store in Newport, Arkansas. He was able to price his products at below average cost by buying wholesale products directly from suppliers. He was fortunate in that his store was centrally located, which made it easier for customers to get to. His store's operating hours were also longer than his competitors and he kept all of his shelves stocked with a variety of products that customers needed and wanted. Through his persistence, dedication and hard work, he was able to triple his business. By 1950, his store was the lead Ben Franklin variety store in 6 states. At that point, his landlord became interested in the business and offered to buy him out. His lease was not renewed when he refused to sell the store.

Sam Walton didn't give up. He looked for a new place in rural areas around Arkansas. He insisted on a 99-year lease in a place he found in Bentonville, Arkansas near the town square. During the summer of that year, he opened Walton's Five and Dime store. He employed the same strategy; he offered consistently low prices, kept longer operating hours than his competitors and kept his shelves stocked with a variety of products. His store became a success. Naturally, he started looking for more opportunities.

He started buying more Ben Franklin variety stores using profits from his stores and borrowing money as well. He also sought out top-notch managers from other retail and variety stores and convinced them to work for him as managers and he encouraged them to invest for reasonable equity in the business so that by 1962, he and his brother owned 16 stores throughout Arkansas, Missouri and Kansas. However, he wasn't happy with the profits he was getting at that time. So, he implemented a new strategy of dramatically discounting prices to kill his competitors' businesses and make up the price difference through a higher sales volume. He wanted to establish big discount stores in rural areas.

The Birth of Wal-Mart

Walton brought up the idea of cutting prices even more than they previously by operating with higher volume of merchandise to the franchisors of Ben Franklin but it was turned down. Walton and his brother decided to do it themselves. He mortgaged his home and borrowed heavily in order to build his very first Wal-Mart in Rogers, Arkansas in 1962. Although Woolco and Kmart also launched discounting on that same year, these retail giants didn't bother taking notice of Wal-Mart because it was located in rural areas.

Sales soared at Wal-Mart and by 1969 Walton already had 18 stores around Missouri and Arkansas. In 1970, Wal-Mart went public with Walton retaining 61% stock ownership. This strategy allowed him to pay off Wal-Mart's debts and expand.

Wal-Mart had an additional 6 stores when it first went public. On its 2nd and 3rd year, the store had an additional 26 branches. On its 4th and 5th year, another 14 and 16 stores were added, respectively. At the start of 1981, Wal-Mart had grown to 276 stores with a plan to add 100 stores yearly.

Sam's Wholesale Club was first launched in 1983. It was planned to be a wholesale store for small-scale businesses. Sam Walton was named Forbes' Richest Man in America in 1985. His worth was estimated to be $2.8 billion. Wal-Mart grew to become

America's 3rd biggest retailer after Sears and Kmart. In 1988, he gave up his CEO position to David Glass but retained his position as Chairman.

By 1990, Sam Walton was diagnosed with bone cancer. However, due to his competitive spirit, he told investors at the company's annual meeting that Wal-Mart will be able to reach revenue of $125 billion before year 2000. In 1992, Wal-Mart became America's biggest retail store. In March of that year, US President George Bush awarded Sam Walton with Medal of Freedom because of his unwavering entrepreneurial spirit and concern for his workers and community. On March 19, two days after the awarding ceremony, Sam Walton was admitted to the University Of Arkansas Hospital. He died on April 5, 1992 with a net worth of almost $25 billion.

The Ten Commandments According Sam Walton

- Stay committed to the business.
- Profits must be shared with associates and they must be treated as partners.
- Colleagues must be energized.
- Open communication to partners is important.
- Show appreciation to associates.
- Success should be celebrated.
- Keep ears open to everyone within the firm.
- Expectations of customers must be exceeded.
- Better expense control must be observed than the competitors.
- Own path should be blazed.

The Reasons for Wal-Mart's Success

Wal-Mart was successful because it was open to the quick adoption of technology. Sam Walton knew he had to keep costs down in order to keep profits up. He did this by keeping tight control on inventory. He ordered the right amount of inventory at the right time. He realized that if the store had a lot of inventory, he would have to pay for those items even if they were just stocked in the warehouse.

On the other hand, if the store kept too little inventory, sales would be lost. So, he purchased electronic scanners and used them at the cash registers which were then linked to a system of inventory control. With this system, Wal-Mart was able to reorder fast moving items at the right quantities in order to restock its shelves to prevent lost sales.

Sam Walton didn't invent retailing. He created innovations that made the business more efficient and profitable.

Sam Walton refused to yield. When he started his retail business, he couldn't get a loan from a bank. His suppliers demanded cash for every delivery. In fact, he had to pay for the products prior to shipment. Sam Walton persevered. He had to overcome multiple hardships in order to succeed. He was able to grow his business to the point where it would become the world's largest retail store; thus making him the world's richest man during his time.

Sam Walton took smart risk. He had a unique vision and saw I through. He didn't take the path others had taken. He became a trail blazer. He kept people who continuously challenged the way he thought. He liked to be in the company of people who were not afraid to speak their mind. He continuously searched for ways and means to change the status quo. Many regarded him as a maverick. He was headstrong, but he was also fair. He enjoyed debates and encouraged his people to take risks.

He admitted to failing 9 out of 10 times but in the end he succeeded which made it all the more gratifying. He believed that companies had to take the risks in order to be different from their competitors. He even encouraged business owners to sometimes go the opposite direction. There one might succeed when everyone fails.

Although there were some who believed that Sam Walton was simply lucky, that he gambled on his idea and won. However, Walton was quick to refute that theory. He said he believed in managing risks. He didn't gamble. His strategy was different from big retailers when he first started Wal-Mart in 1962. He focused on rural areas while his competitors concentrated on urban areas. Walton raised the standard of living in the rural areas. His "rural retailing" was considered radical at that time.

Think about it. He opened large stores in small rural areas. No one did that. Yet, people within a 50-mile radius trooped to his stores. His strategy on rural discounting worked and because of its success, he used that same strategy when he expanded into urban areas.

Wal-Mart after Sam Walton's Death

When Sam Walton died, his eldest son succeeded him as Chairman. Wal-Mart already had stores in 45 states and plans were being prepared to expand to Puerto Rico, Oregon, Montana, and Idaho. The following year, Bobby Martin was chosen as President of the newly created Wal-Mart International Division. The retail store also expanded to Washington, Rhode Island, Hawaii, and Alaska. By the end of 1993, Wal-Mart had already achieved sales beyond the billion-dollar mark.

In 1994, Wal-Mart acquired Kmart's 91 PACE Membership Warehouse. In Canada, it acquired 122 Woolco stores. It also opened 96 stores in Mexico and 3 Value Clubs in Hong Kong. By 1995, Wal-Mart had grown to $93.6 billion in sales with 276 international stores, 433 Sam's Clubs, 239 Supercenters, and 1,995 Discount Stores. Associates had grown to 675,000. Wal-Mart expanded to Brazil, Argentina, and Vermont, USA.

Wal-Mart partook a joint venture agreement in 1996 so that it could enter China. It went public in 1997 and replaced Woolworth at the Dow Jones. It also acquired stores in Germany. A year later, it acquired 4 Korea Makro stores in South Korea. In 1999, UK's Asda Stores Ltd. chain became a subsidiary of Wal-Mart. By 2000, sales in the United States of America had grown to $156 billion and Lee Scott became CEO and President.

By 2005, Wal-Mart had reached sales of $312.4 billion with at least 6,200 stores worldwide and at least 1.6 million associates. It also had presence in countries like Costa Rica, Nicaragua, Honduras, El Salvador, and Guatemala. In 2011, Wal-Mart acquired majority of the shares of Massmart Holdings providing access to Zambia, Uganda,

Tanzania, Swaziland, Nigeria, Namibia, Mozambique, Mauritius, Malawi, Lesotho, Ghana, Botswana, and South Africa.

Lessons from the Life of Sam Walton

Sam Walton strived for excellence in everything that he did. He questioned the status quo and made efforts to change it for the better. He never stopped searching for new ways to do things. He knew that he had to be innovative if his business was to succeed. He was not afraid of taking risks, because he was never fearful to failure. His perseverance paid off.

Sam Walton relished challenges. He always asked questions. He wanted to conquer every obstacle that came his way and he never lost focus on what he wanted to accomplish. He was able to bring Wal-Mart to the top and made him one of the most successful entrepreneurs that the United States has ever had. When he died, he left a legacy. People must learn from the life of Sam Walton. It was his innovation and perseverance which made Wal-Mart the top retail store in the market.

ROSALIA MERA

World's Wealthiest Self-made Woman

Considered as Spain's wealthiest woman, Rosalia Mera stopped schooling to become a dress shop seamstress at age 11. Her work at La Maja was very good so she was promoted as sales assistant. When she married Amancio Ortega, the couple converted their living room to a dress shop where lingerie and gowns were made. Inditex was built by the husband and wife team and became a fashion empire, famous around the world for its Zara brand although the empire also carried brands like Uterque, Zara Home, Pull & Bear, Massimo Duti, Oysho, and Bershka. She died of stroke complications at age 69 in August 2013 during her vacation in Menorca with Sandra, her daughter. When she died he had 5.1% stake in the company and had donated money to marine fish farming, cancer treatment research, and to a newborn fingerprinting system company.

Early Life of Rosalia Mera

Rosalia Mera Goyenechea was born on January 28, 1944 in La Coruña, Spain. Her father was an employee of an electricity company. Her mother was the manager of a butcher shop. She married her husband, Amancio Ortega Gaona, a messenger, when she was 22. Rosalia Mera already had her GOA homemade dress company when she met her husband.

She built Zara with her husband in 1975. Today, the brand is known all over the world and is considered the biggest fashion retailer. The 1st Zara store was opened in La Coruña in 1975. The brand's strategy was quickly imitating popular known brands and selling the merchandise inexpensively.

The Growth of Rosalia Mera's Career

Inditex was built in 1985 as a holding company because the husband and wife team had built other businesses as well, although Zara remained its flagship. It has at least 120,000 employees and at least 6,000 stores in at least 86 countries. When the couple divorced in 1986, she retained 7% stake in Inditex. She was known to fund

Zeltia, a company focused on researching on cancer treatments using natural and synthetic compounds. She was listed as Spain's 2nd wealthiest person after her ex-husband. She was estimated to have a net worth of at least $6 billion.

Rosalia Mera's Other Activities

Rosalia Mera was a known supporter of relaxed abortion laws in Spain. She opposed any budget cuts on education and health care. She formed Paideia Galiza Foundation which is known to work with those people at risk of social exclusion.

How the Zara Brand Became a Global Brand

Today, Zara is estimated to have global presence in 86 countries, with 1,750 retail shops. It became successful by adapting the latest and coolest high-end fashion and selling the clothes at affordable prices. The clothes are made within 2 weeks and sold in high-end outlets. Zara is able to come up with different designs and styles every few weeks.

The husband and wife team was able to offer the Zara clothes at inexpensive prices because they kept production in their seamstresses' homes in Galicia. The seamstresses' wages were low because Galicia is a poor region in Spain. Some production was also outsourced to Portugal. The Zara brand was able to change lines quickly because the design to production activities was kept local. Its competitors were outsourcing their production to Asian countries. Timing was also right when the couple opened its first Zara store. Spanish dictator Franco had just died and a lot of Spaniards were interested in well-cut, modern, and colorful clothes.

From La Coruña, Zara expanded to Portugal by 1988 and then to London, Paris, and New York. Although the company had made the couple billionaires, Inditex and Zara continue to be headquartered in La Coruña.

The apparel industry was transformed by Zara because it sped up the response of the mass market to high fashion designs. Zara introduced variations to the high-end designs from fashion houses and sold them in retail stores within 2 weeks. In recent years, it took 6 months for high-end fashion to be copied and sold in the market. This was made possible through vertical integration. The Duchess of Cambridge, Kate Middleton, is a known patron of Zara.

What sets Zara from its competitors is the brand's willingness to listen to its customers. Customers can suggest variations to a design. Zara will have it in stores in just a matter of days. Inditex went public in 2001 and Louis Vuitton fashion director Daniel Piette was quoted as saying that the company may be the most devastating yet most innovative retailer around the world.

The name Zara wasn't the first choice of the couple. They really wanted to call their clothing store Zorba, an inspiration which came from the "Zorba the Greek" film. However, they found out that Zorba was already the name of a bar near their home. So, they settled for Zara instead because they already had the molds ready for the storefront sign.

The Life of Rosalia Mera after Her Divorce

When she got divorced in 1986, Rosalia Mera no longer had any direct interest in the company. She, however, still maintained some shares in the company in order to maintain her position in the list of world's wealthiest women.

She focused on humanitarian causes like her foundation which aims to search for means to integrate physically or mentally disabled people by searching jobs for them. It is said this cause is something close to her heart because her son Marcos has a mental disability. She has a large investment in London's Bulgari Hotel in order to finance her humanitarian advocacies.

Lessons Learned From Rosalia Mera

For Rosalia Mera, her poverty wasn't a hindrance. She may have stopped schooling at a young age to work but this didn't stop her from attaining her goals. She perfected her craft and came up with lingerie designs which were ahead of its time. Yet, the pieces of lingerie were patronized by the Spanish ladies. She wasn't afraid of the challenges ahead. Instead of being scared, she faced the challenges head on. She worked hard to realize her dreams.

Secondly, Rosalia Mera knew how to innovate. When she put up Zara, she knew she had to offer something different. Thus, she sped up the design-to-store process and was able to sell variations of high-end designs within two weeks at a cheaper price. She learned to deal with people well. She kept them happy so their workers continued working for them. By cutting the amount of time it takes to produce replicas of high-end fashion, Zara's loyal clientele grew and had included people from different parts of the globe.

Thirdly, Rosalia Mera knew how to give back to society. She organized a foundation and became an angel investor to new and struggling companies. She was also vocal about political issues and strived to make a difference. Instead of keeping quiet and being reclusive, Rosalia Mera chose to live her life after her stint at Inditex to the fullest. She really made a 180-degree turn for the better.

Rosalia Mera is a woman, a self-made woman with a heart for the underprivileged. She worked hard and she was rewarded for all her efforts. Everyone can be like her. Nothing is impossible. If she did it, anybody can.

URSULA M. BURNS

Her success Story

The story of Ursula M. Burns is a typical rags-to-riches story. She lived with her mom in New York City. Her life in the housing project, The Baruch Houses, was formed by her mother's values, her knack in mathematics and science, her trust in herself, and hard work. She was reported to have earned at least $13 million as CEO and Chairwoman of Xerox in 2010. She was appointed by no less than the US President to the Science, Technology, Engineering, and Math (STEM) project and as co-chair of the Export Council.

Lessons Ursula M. Burns Learned From Her Mother

Being a single mother with 3 children to provide for, Olga worked odd jobs. She did babysitting, cleaning, and laundry chores in her neighborhood. She taught her kids about success and of being good to people. She encouraged them to be forever curious and learn. She taught them to always act accordingly and do their best at all times. She inspired them to be good citizens and be a winner every time. She told them not to worry about things that they can't control.

The Education of Ursula M. Burns

Ursula M. Burns studied basic education at the Cathedral High on East 56th Street. Her siblings urged her to study Education in college but she wanted to be more financially able. She researched at the library and looked for jobs which paid well and used a lot of math and science. She started with Chemical Engineering but decided to pursue and finish a course in Mechanical Engineering at the Polytechnic Institute of New York in 1980. She had her Master's degree right after from Columbia University.

How She Began Work at Xerox

She worked as an intern at Xerox during college and was hired right after graduation. She was assigned to product development and planning for 10 years. She was asked to join the work-life session being handled by the company's senior executive, Wayland Hicks. She became an executive assistant of Hicks because he noticed her curiosity about a lot of things. She was mentored by him and was often part of executive meetings as well.

She was made executive assistant of the president, Paul Allaire, when he noticed the same curiosity Wayland Hicks noticed about her. She raised a hand and asked him a question in one of the meetings presided by Allaire. She was mentored by most of the executives of the company. She was made VP for global manufacturing in 1999. She was prepared to leave Xerox in 2000 when the company experienced problems and turmoil. However, she was encouraged to stay by the company's board of directors. She led the group in Corporate Strategic Services as senior vice president and worked with Ms. Anne Mulcahy in turning the company around.

Ursula Burns became the president of Xerox in 2007. She was made Chief Executive Officer in 2009. The following year, she also became Chairwoman. She holds the distinction of being the first African-American woman to become Chief Executive Officer of a Fortune 500 company. Ms. Burns is also part of different professional and community boards such as the RUMP Group, the Rochester Business Alliance, the MIT Corporation, the University of Rochester, the National Association of Manufacturers, FIRST, Boston Scientific, and American Express. In 2009, she was named as 14th most powerful woman by Forbes.

4-time Forbes' Power Women

Since Ms. Burns became CEO of Xerox, she was named into Forbes' Power Women for four times already. In October 2010, the first time she was included in the roster, Ursula M. Burns was cited for her role as CEO in acquiring Affiliated Computer Services. The deal which cost Xerox $6.4 billion was followed by a deal with California Medicaid for $1.6 billion which paved the way for 9.7% increase in the share price of Xerox. She is believed to be transforming Xerox to become a data service company.

In August 2011, Forbes included Ms. Burns in the Power Women list again. Ursula M. Burns was credited for Xerox's transformation into a services-driven company which also included management of parking meters, road tolls, and electronic ticket transactions. She was also cited for leading the Science, Technology, Engineering, and Math program of the White House as well as being vice-chair of the Export Council.

In August 2012, Ms. Burns was again named as Forbes' Power women. She was credited for continuously transforming Xerox into the services businesses with acquisitions of processing and health care technologies. Half of the total revenues of Xerox were said to have come from services. She was also quoted as saying that the all-male membership of the Augusta National Golf Club was "ridiculous" and that her company won't be sponsoring the Masters if the policy remained unchanged. The golf club finally accepted women to the club after 80 years of being an all-male golf club. Darla Moore, a South Carolina financier, and Condoleezza Rice became the club's first female members.

Ms. Burns was also named into Forbes' Power Women last May 2013. Total revenue of Xerox has continuously grown under her watch. For 2012, at least half of Xerox's $22.4 billion revenues were from IT services. Xerox is expected to continue acquiring data analytics companies to further strengthen its businesses in health care not only in the United States of America but in other countries as well.

Advice from Ursula M. Burns

When Ms. Burns was asked for advice to young women, she told them to seek an older yet good husband because the man had already grown up and the difference in age is advantageous because the woman can advance her career when the husband is already retired and can take care of the children at home. Ms. Burns is married to Lloyd Bean, a researcher and scientist at Xerox and is older by 20 years.

According to her, there must be a redefinition of work-life balance and that women should seek balance during their entire life. Also, she said that women should take care of their personal needs over family and career. These women should take care not only of their physical health but of their mental health as well. They shouldn't be guilty when they miss some of their children's activities because "Kids are pretty resilient."

Lastly, Ms. Burns said life shouldn't be taken seriously. Women shouldn't be crazy about life because 90% of it isn't serious. What is important, though, is that women must be prudent and go back to the basics. Life is meant to be enjoyed. Problems may come but it important for women to keep their center. They should see these problems as temporary roadblocks that should be hurdled in order to reach their goals. Problems don't have to keep women off the tracks. They should persevere in order to realize their dreams.

The life of Ursula M. Burns is a living testament that race, sex and financial conditions shouldn't be a stumbling block in the realization of one's goals. She persevered against all odds and she triumphed. Let her life be a guiding example to each and every one that people who persevered often become successful.

SYLVESTER STALLONE

How He Became Successful

If there's a tale of real rags-to-riches, it must be the story of Sylvester Stallone. He was able to defy every impossible situation so that he can enjoy the fame and fortune he is experiencing today. His life story is really inspirational as it is phenomenal as well. He has proven to each and every one that it is possible for committed individuals to turn their lives around.

Early Years in the Life of Sylvester Stallone

Sylvester Stallone's real name is Michael Sylvester Gardenzio Stallone, who was born to an Italian father and Russian Jewish-French mother. He was born in 1946 and is known as an American actor, film director, and scriptwriter. He is world renowned for his portrayals of John Rambo and Rocky Balboa. He has a younger brother who is an actor/musician.

The props used in "Rocky" had been kept at the Smithsonian Museum while the film itself was enlisted to the National Film Registry. A statue of "Rocky" is also prominently displayed near the Philadelphia Museum of Art.

Only a few people know the life story of Sylvester Stallone. A part of his face is paralyzed because of complications during his birth. His chin, lip, and tongue are affected. This is the reason why people may have noticed his slurred speech.

Because his parents fought a lot until he was 5 years old, he had to stay in foster homes in Hell's Kitchen located in New York. He struggled through his early life, often getting suspended due to behavioral dilemmas, poor grades, and frequent fights. His parents eventually got divorced when he was 9 and had since lived with his mother.

Sylvester Stallone started schooling in suburban Philadelphia. He began acting there but moved to Geneva, Switzerland to teach at an American college for 2 years. He began taking drama at the

University of Miami when he got back. He also started writing at the same time.

Stallone didn't finish college because he decided to try acting as a career in New York. He wasn't able to land an acting stint even though he auditioned relentlessly to most casting agents. It was then that he decided to focus on writing screenplays.

Sylvester Stallone's Early Career in Hollywood

In 1970, Stallone starred in "The Party at Kitty and Stud's", a soft core porn film wherein he received $200 for his work. He said he did it because he had been booted out of his apartment and he became homeless for a few days. He had slept at the New York City Port Authority for 3 weeks. The film was, however, released as "Italian Stallion" when he became famous. He was also part of Score, an erotic stage play in 1971 which was staged at Martinique Theatre.

He also appeared in "No Place To Hide" in 1970 which was later recut and relabeled as "Rebel" where Stallone was the star. In 1990, the film was later reedited with newly shot scenes and shown as a parody entitled "A Man Called... Rainbo".

Sylvester Stallone landed minor roles from 1971 to 1975. He landed a major role in "The Lords of Flatbush" in 1974 where he also wrote additional dialogues worthy of receiving a credit. After the film, he started struggling again. Instead of becoming depressed, he wrote more screenplays. His situation became desperate because he couldn't even provide for his family.

He accidentally entered a library when he was walking the New York streets in order to keep warm. It was there that he began reading the works of Edgar Allan Poe and Tolstoy. This experience gave him a small edge against other writers. He was desperate for work but he only wanted jobs as an actor because he knew it was his destiny.

How "Rocky" Came To Be

Sylvester Stallone got the idea of "Rocky" while he was watching the Muhammad Ali-Chuck Wepner fight at home. He noticed that Wepner didn't give up easily even though he was absolutely on the losing end. He kept on fighting till the end. This inspiration kept Stallone up for at least 24 hours so that he could finish the "Rocky" script. He approached a lot of producers but each one of them rejected his screenplay.

His destitute situation drove Stallone to sell his dog to someone outside a liquor store. His dog was his best friend but he had to sell it for $50 so he could have money. What's remarkable about Sylvester Stallone was his determination to sell the "Rocky" screenplay. He didn't stop peddling the story to every producer.

One day, a producer got interested in his screenplay. Stallone got so excited and told him that he wants to play "Rocky". The producer declined to give the role to Stallone so the latter declined the producer's $100,000 offer. The producer returned a few weeks after and offered a higher price for the screenplay but Stallone was adamant. He wanted to play the lead role. The offer reached $400,000 but he still didn't want to sell his screenplay.

The producer offered $25,000 for both the screenplay and Stallone's portrayal of the lead role. Sylvester Stallone accepted the offer. He went back to the liquor store to wait for the stranger who bought his dog to come by. The stranger came on the 3rd day. Stallone offered $150 for his dog but the stranger didn't want to sell the dog. He raised the offer to $15,000 plus a role in "Rocky". The stranger agreed.

The Challenges in Filming "Rocky"

United Artists planned on casting James Caan, Burt Reynolds, Ryan O'Neal, or Robert Redford as "Rocky" but Sylvester Stallone wouldn't have it any other way. He had to be "Rocky". The original script had to be modified because the character of Mickey was supposed to be a racist. Also, the original ending was different. Rocky threw the fight away because he realized he didn't like professional boxing.

The producers were hesitant to award the lead role to Stallone because he was an unknown in the field. Those who were first tapped to play Apollo Creed and Adrian backed out. Ken Norton backed out and Carl Weathers took his role as Apollo Creed. Carrie Snodgress was chosen to play Adrian but negotiations didn't push through because of money dispute. The role eventually went to Talia Shire.

Both Carl Weathers and Sylvester Stallone suffered injuries during the shooting of "Rocky". Weathers had a damaged nose while Stallone had bruised ribs. The budget for the whole production of the film was $1,075,000, with an additional $4.2 million for advertising and $100,000 for producers' fees. "Rocky", however, grossed at least $225 million worldwide. It holds the distinction of having the 7th highest gross to budget ratio.

The Lessons in the Life of Sylvester Stallone

The success of Stallone teaches everyone that each individual can overcome every hardship he is experiencing. Every person is equipped to achieve his life's goals regardless of gender, race, age, or educational background. Persistence is the key if an individual wants to succeed.

Just like Sylvester Stallone, each person mustn't give up on his dreams. If it is really his heart's desire, he must strive really hard in order to make his dreams a reality. Sure, there will be so many distractions but he must remain focused on achieving his goals in life. Each disappointment must be seen not as a setback but as a challenge to try harder.

What's also remarkable about Stallone is that he believed in himself. He kept trying until he became successful. While waiting for his acting career to flourish, he perfected another craft: scriptwriting. His "Rocky" screenplay is his springboard to jumpstart his lifelong dream of becoming an actor.

Everyone can be Sylvester Stallone. Each individual can learn new things in preparation for his dream. He shouldn't sit around and wait for opportunities to come. He must be prepared for the coming opportunities by creating a better person of himself so that when his big chance comes he is ready, just like Stallone. He mustn't settle for anything less than what his heart desires.

Sylvester Stallone experienced a lot of difficulties. He had been evicted from his rented apartment. He slept at the port for 3 weeks! He was penniless but the experience didn't kill his enthusiasm. He was still determined to make it big in Hollywood.

A person may experience difficulties in life. He may lose a loved one. He may be evicted like Stallone. He may be forced to take lowly jobs just to get by. But, everything will pass. Things will get better. The sun will always shine the next morning. Therefore, everybody shouldn't lose hope. Even if it's just a glimmer of hope today, things will surely be better.

Tomorrow is another day. It doesn't always rain. There's always a rainbow after the rain, a promise that life will get better soon. No one has a monopoly of all the hardships and difficulties in life. Out there, there's somebody who has more sufferings and heartaches. Thus, each person must keep a positive outlook.

How Jay-Z Became Successful

Born as Shawn Corey Carter, Jay-Z is first and foremost an A merican rapper who has ventured into record producing and other bus inesses. Forbes estimated his net worth to be about $500 million in 20 12. During his career, he sold about 500 million albums across the wo rld and won 17 Grammies for his work. He is considered to be one of the best rappers. In 2006, MTV ranked him as #1 in "The Greatest M Cs of All Time".

Jay-Z is also known to be part-creator of Rocawear and part-o wner of 40/40 Club. He founded Roc Nation and co-founded Roc-a-F ella Records. He was also CEO of Def Jam Recordings. He is a certifi ed sports agent of MLB and NBA, and also founder of Roc Nation Sp orts. He is married to the equally famous R&B singer Beyonce with whom he has 1 daughter.

Early Life of Jay-Z

Jay-Z spent his childhood at Marcy Houses in Brooklyn, New York. His mother Gloria singlehandedly took care of him and his 3 si blings when his father abandoned them. In one of his songs, he said th at he stole his older brother's jewelry when he was 12 by shooting the latter's shoulder.

He went to Eli Whitney High School with AZ, a future rapper like him. When the school was closed down, he transferred to George Westinghouse Career and Technical Education High School with futu re rappers Busta Rhymes and The Notorious B.I.G. He also moved to Trenton Central High School but he didn't finish high school. In his s ongs, he said he sold crack cocaine and been shot 3 times.

In the words of her mother, Jay-Z would use the kitchen table as his drums which would eventually wake up his siblings in the midd le of the night. On his birthday, his mother gifted him a boom box wh ich paved the way for his inclination towards music. He wrote lyrics a nd began free styling. He would follow famous artists during that tim e. Jay-Z got his name because his neighbors used to call him as "Jazz y". The name was also in honor of Jaz-O who became Jay-Z's musical mentor. In July of this year, Jay-Z announced that he now wants to be known as Jay Z.

The Beginning of Jay-Z's Musical Career

Jay-Z's voice had a small participation in the early recordings of Jaz-O, including "Hawaiian Sophie" and "The Originators". Jay-Z also had won different contests with rapper LL Cool J so that he can win a record deal. He was featured in "Show and Prove" in Daddy's H ome, an album of Big Daddy Kane in 1994. During this time, he was referred as the hype man of Big Daddy Kane. He also appeared on "D a Graveyard", a famous song by Big L, and "Time to Build" of Mic G eronimo in 1995. Jay-Z's rap single was "In My Lifetime" which also had a music video.

Decoder: Jay-Z's autobiography

Jay-Z wrote his autobiography and is set to be released on Nov ember 16. However, every page of Decoder will be released before it is made available in bookstores. In this book, Jay-Z is said to talk abo ut his past including allegations of being a hustler, of stabbings, and o f drug selling. It also talks about his grouchy relationships with other rap artists like MC Hammer.

Jay-Z is said to have been gifted by his mother with a 3-ring bi nder in which he wrote down rhymes about anything under the sun. T he notebook was always hidden under his bed at night so that nobody can steal it. In order to use more words in his rhymes, he began readin g the dictionary. Before high school, he was already joining rap conte sts within the neighborhood so that he could become the "best poet on the block".

His father, Adnis Reeves, left the family when he was 11 years old. Although he attended different high schools in Brooklyn, Jay-Z d id well in school even though he rarely studied. However, he dropped out of school and dealt crack.

He started dealing drugs because of his neighbors. He saw kid s selling crack so they could pay their electric bills at their homes. Th ose kids were equipped with firearms. When Jay-Z was 13 years old, he started with crack and even had his own group in Trenton, New Jer sey and Maryland. He didn't stop writing rhymes while he sold crack t o earn a living.

When he was 16, Jay-Z was arrested for dealing crack in Trent on. He was caught when he visited "Hill", his friend, at a high school there. He had crack inside his pockets. Because it was his first arrest, he wasn't put to jail but the crack was confiscated. So that he can pay his crack supplier he dealt crack in his old neighborhood for 2 1/2 day s. To keep him awake, he wrote rhymes and ate cookies.

Jay-Z continued dealing crack. He and his group conquered Ea st Coast, searching for drug suppliers and selling crack. In 1994, he h ad drugs inside his Maxima's fake compartment when he was apprehe nded by the police. Because the cops can't search his car, they had to wait for the K-9 unit which arrived late so Jay-Z was able to go scot f ree.

Whenever he would visit New York, Jay-Z always made sure he met Jaz, his friend, who was also a rhymer. They would spend a lo t of time writing rhymes. In 1989, EMI signed up Jaz for a record deal but the single flopped so his friend was dropped. In 1994, Jay-Z starte d Roc-a-fella, his own label, with Kareem "Biggs" Burke and Damon Dash.

In 1998, Jay-Z became a breakout star with "Hard Knock Life ", which he lifted from Little Orphan Annie. At first, he was turned d own by the "Annie" franchise when he asked for permission to use th e chorus in his song. He wrote a letter to the company and lied that he won an essay contest in 7th grade where the prize was a ticket to see " Annie". The franchise eventually agreed and a "Hard Knock Life" wa s his 1st mega-hit.

According to Jay-Z, hip-hop stars like him often suffer from t he hands of fellow hip-hop stars, especially when they become popula

r. Tupac Shakur and The Notorious B.I.G. were killed when they wer e at their peak. In 2003, when he met Eminem to record for his single "Moment of Clarity", the latter had a bulletproof vest on.

In 1994, Jay-Z was introduced by Biggie to Cristal Champagn e. He included the drink's name in his rhymes. When a reporter asked Frederic Rouzad, managing director of Cristal, if he thinks the brand may have been compromised because it is being associated with the " bling lifestyle", Rouzad said that they can't prevent people from purch asing it. So, Jay-Z began to boycott Cristal Champagne.

With regards to the 1999 incident when he stabbed Lance Riv era, a record producer, he said he had to plead guilty to assault wherei n he got 3 years probation. He said he was furious when he learned so mebody leaked a copy of "Volume 3: Life and Times of S. Carter" at l east 1 month before its release. He said he receive word that it was Ri vera who leaked it. So, when he saw Lance Rivera at the Kit Kat Klub for the release of Q-Tip's album, he got so mad after he confronted hi m. Rivera went to the police to complain about Jay-Z. He pleaded gui lty because Puff Daddy had been acquitted previously and he felt that the state would make it harder for him to avenge its loss in Puff Dadd y's case.

In "Moment of Clarity", it talked about his father's abandonme nt of the family when he was 11. It was only much later that he realiz ed his father resulted to alcohol when his brother's killers had not bee n caught by the police. He became obsessed with finding the killers w hich also led to the failure of his marriage. Jay-Z reunited with his fat her because his mother urged him. In 2003, his father died because of a liver disease.

In 2008, Jay-Z met with President Obama and realized that he was called so that the President could understand how people like him think politically. At Obama's inauguration, Jay-Z was watching from t he audience so that he could feel how everyday people felt about the President.

Who is Jay-Z off Stage?

Jay-Z is still a poet even in his everyday speech. He would oft en deliver aphorisms with rhetorical flair, reflecting hard-earned wisd om. He said he'd managed to be true to himself and not impress other people. Jay-Z sold about 40 million albums and built a business empir e. He realized that people will continuously patronize him and his bus inesses if they are convinced whatever they purchase reflects the true Jay-Z.

For Jay-Z, his brands are his extensions so he has to remain tr ue because what he truly feels is reflected to his brands. In everyday c onversations, Jay-Z doesn't break into incendiary raps. His speech is o ften deliberate, calmer, and slower. He is an animated and engaged tal ker. If he wants to emphasize something he's saying, he'd be quick to t ouch the other person in a friendly way.

Jay-Z may seem accessible and laid back but he's also confide nt. He's congenial and cooperative but he's often surrounded by peopl e who are ready to be of service to him. His manner is easy going whi ch allowed him to move in and out of different exclusive circles and c ross cultural boundaries.

When he was growing up, no one ever thought Jay-Z can be s o successful although people who knew him often describe him as bri ght or smart. He identified sports figures as his 1st success models be cause athletes often came from where he came from. He could relate t o his sports heroes. While he could relate to athletes, he also found hi p-hop. He wrote rhymes on notebooks and kept his family awake whe n he used their kitchen table as his drums. He connected with Jaz-O a nd even recorded with him and Big Daddy Kane. Although these peo ple realized his talent, Jay-Z wasn't ready to give up his drug dealing because he was making a lot of money through it.

When he decided he wanted to try hip-hop, record companies didn't want to sign him up. Therefore, he put up his own record label, Roc-a-Fella Records. Reasonable Doubt was released in 1996. He dec ided to concentrate on hip-hop and establish his business empire. He r

ealized that the music industry is a completely different world than th
e one he decided to leave behind.

Jay-Z's record label Roc-A-Fella is a bragging right which con
nects a budding rapper to the most powerful and richest families in th
e history of America. It also served as a means from which he would
build his businesses. Families like the Rockefeller had a monopoly of
the products they produced. This was how the career of Jay-Z develop
ed all through the years he's in the music industry. He created a marke
t not only for his music but for his lifestyle as well.

Jay-Z is of the belief that hip-hop has aspirational power. He b
elieves that his fans want him to succeed so that they can emulate him
. For him, rock and roll stars dislike success and business. They hid th
eir success from the public although their followers know how much t
hey're really worth. However, for hip-hop, its aim is to amass wealth.
Fans respect their hip-hop idols because of their success. Different ki
nds of people are drawn to successful hip-hop stars even though they
don't like hip-hop.

With regards to credibility, Jay-Z said that it's an insecure emo
tion. He said he doesn't go to the projects anymore because he had to i
nspire those people in the projects to get out. He wasn't really immun
e from insecurities. He stabbed Lance Rivera in 1999 and was charge
d with loaded handgun possession in 2001. He pleaded guilty to the a
ssault case while the gun possession case was dropped.

In general, people had observed that these incidents with possi
ble jail time proved to be enough for Jay-Z to shy away from the life
of a thug. He had lyrics which talked about the arrests but those rhym
es were no longer transformed into real life thus ending the life he use
d to live. Although fellow rappers had taunted him "Gay-Z" in their ra
ps but Jay-Z never bothered to confront them. He shied away from riv
alries because he didn't want the deaths of The Notorious B.I.G. and
Tupac Shakur to happen again.

Jay-Z can no longer risk his life, his bling, or his money. He is
already old enough to know about hip-hop's cultural impact as well as

his critical role in it. He said that hip-hop has done a lot for racial rela tions and it must be accorded the necessary credit. Hip-hop caused im mense transformation in the United States of America. In fact, Jay-Z believed that it had done more than anyone to change race relations.

According to him, children learn racism at home because whe n one is already a teenager, he won't be able to learn racism because h e would be idolizing somebody like Snoop Dogg and listen to rap mu sic. Therefore, it would be difficult for the teenager to be taught racis m. Jay-Z further added that the least racist generation is the current ge neration who listens to rap music. Hip-hop music has gone worldwide and people intermingle and have fun with each other.

In Jay-Z's view, hip-hop was also instrumental in electing US President Barack Obama. Jay-Z helped during Obama's campaign by appearing on various concert venues and recording a message for Afri can-American voters. In an interview, Jay-Z said that politics never ca me to areas where he grew up but Obama's camp reached out to him t o ask for his help during the campaign.

Jay-Z is a sharp businessman as well. Although a lot of people think that he's just a front man or a figurehead, he is very serious abou t his businesses. Like in his music, Jay-Z is also full of determination in his business enterprise. He has a clear vision yet he has the willing ness to listen to other people. He keeps his people motivated. He's loo king into long term goals instead of short-term gains. He insists on sta ying to his game plan even though the economic situation isn't very id eal. He doesn't want to make changes now when he's not sure if it's go ing to turn out well for his brands.

Who Is Jay-Z To Other People?

In the words of Iconix Brand Group CEO and Chairman Neil Cole, Jay-Z is "smart as hell". Iconix bought Rocawear from Jay-Z fo r at least $200 million. Cole said that Jay-Z understands that he is the brand, a very well thought out brand. The latter has weekly meetings so he doesn't decide on impulse. He isn't willing to settle and very con sistent too. Everything must feel right for Jay-Z. Otherwise, he won't do it even if it will bring him a lot of money. He is willing to wait for the right time. His taste is wonderful and he knows where to take his brands as well as himself.

Live Nation CEO and President Michael Rapino also said the same thing. He said some stars often ask how much money they'll get in potential deals so the cooperation often doesn't flourish because of this. With Jay-Z, money became the topic on their 7th meeting. Rapino said that for Jay-Z, winning isn't everything. The integrity of the win is also important. Rapino considers him a true partner who's always seeking win-win situations.

Jay-Z's vision of success extends far beyond his music and business. He wants to make a meaningful life. Jay-Z is excited to learn. He wants his life to get brighter each day just like Muhammad Ali, Martin Luther King, and Gandhi. Jay-Z believes that each one must strive to have a meaningful life.

Jay-Z's Interview for Vanity Fair

Jay-Z had an interview with Lisa Robinson, contributing editor of Vanity Fair. According to him, Blue Ivy likes to listen to her mother Beyonce's music. In fact, she watches her mother's concerts each night on the computer. Jay-Z said he doesn't play his music in their house but they played his new album and his daughter seemed to like his songs. He said that even if no one bought his Magna Carta album, it's still ok because his daughter Blue Ivy liked it very much.

Jay-Z told Robinson that the 2008 election of US President Obama renewed his American spirit. He said he never imagined a black person can be president that even fellow African-Americans in his housing project neighborhood never thought it was possible. He also said that his mother knew he was into drug dealing when he was young. They never discussed about it. In fact, they ignored it but his mother knew. He said it was normal for mothers to know such things in the neighborhood where he grew up.

Having a checkered past proved to be beneficial for Jay-Z. Be cause he was a drug dealer, he knew about budgets. This knowledge c ame in handy now that he's a sports agent. Living life in that kind of n eighborhood meant that he had to think about an exit strategy. He will either die or get locked up if he didn't get out of that kind of life.

Recalling his childhood, Jay-Z said that they had to make ends meet. They had a tough situation which saw their mother manage the whole family without their father. They were ok. They didn't starve b ut they were struggling. They went to school in the same clothes and dirty sneakers.

Jay-Z said that drugs were everywhere in the neighborhood w here he grew up. Nobody can escape from it. Crack is in the hallway. Crack vials are in the curbs. The putrid smell of crack is in the hallwa ys. Although he got out of the neighborhood, the whole experience is still in his mind.

Jay-Z was never a drug user but he admitted to selling crack. He said he only became guilty that he contributed to the epidemic onl y much later when he realized the effects of crack on the community. However, when he was still selling drugs, his only thoughts were abo ut survival. He thought dealing crack can improve his situation and ca n afford him to buy clothes.

In the 2001 Music Issue of Vanity Fair, Jay-Z and Beyonce w ere just dating. He pursued Beyonce. When asked if he hadn't been Ja y-Z, would he still pursue Beyonce? He said that he probably would i f he's cool. There were rumors that Beyonce wasn't really pregnant wi th Blue Ivy. Jay-Z said that the rumors were stupid.

Jay-Z and Beyonce applied for trademark on their daughter's n ame, Blue Ivy. He said they did it so that other people won't exploit th e name to acquire profit. He said there are people who wanted to use t he name for their products and as parents they don't want people to be nefit from Blue Ivy's name.

With regards to his wealth, he told Robinson that he knows ho w much he actually has up to the last penny but he won't tell anyone.

He said Forbes' estimation of his wealth was just a "guesstimate". He is never motivated by money. He never talks about money with friend s although some of his raps are about it.

With regards to rap, he set his cutoff at 30 years old. But Jay-Z is on his 40s and he's still at it. He said that's how much he loves ra p.

The Mystery of Jay-Z's Brands

Jay-Z was seen riding the train to work. A lot of bloggers blog ged about it, saying that Jay-Z is very much like other average people. Forbes ran an article by Cedric Muhammad who tried to unravel the mystery of Jay-Z and how he stayed relevant until now. According to Muhammad, Jay-Z stayed true to his character. He didn't take assign ments which will force him to veer away from his character. He is als o selective about his interview appearances. He's like Willy Wonka, t he fictional character who stayed reclusive yet delivering popular cho colate products. When Wonka decided to go public, his consumers we nt out of their way to see him.

Jay-Z only had two major missteps in terms of public relations in all his life as a hip-hop icon. He was caught in a word war with Na s, a fellow rap artist, and collaborated with Harry Bellafonte. These w ere just his 2 public relations lapses, according to Muhammad. Jay-Z' s decision to take the train to work is seen as a big deal because he's magnifying his mystery by weaving an illusion of accessibility. Hip-h op icons in the United States of America are considering London and Montreal as their expansion markets. Thus, Jay-Z being seen taking th e train at the London O2 Arena is a clear sign that the man is consider ing taking his brand there.

JOHN D. ROCKEFELLER

The World's Richest Man

Born on July 8, 1839, John D. Rockefeller was credited for Standard Oil, modern philanthropy, and for revolutionizing the oil industry. With an estimated net worth of $663.4 billion, he was said to be the richest man who had ever lived.

Early Life of John D. Rockefeller

Born in Richford, New York, John D. Rockefeller was born to a lumberman and traveling salesman father and a devout Baptist mother. His father, William Avery Rockefeller, had a shady reputation because of his business deals. William was always not at home and even had mistresses aside from John's mother. John's mother, Eliza Davison, taught her children the value of hard work and of being thrifty.

At 16 years old, John D. Rockefeller worked as assistant bookkeeper at 50 cents daily at Hewitt & Tuttle, a small produce commission company. He worked hard and learned how to compute transportation costs. With Maurice B. Clark, he established his first business in 1859. The company was into commission business of meats, grain, and hay deals. He started his 1st oil refinery in 1863 near Cleveland, Ohio.

John Rockefeller married Laura Celestia Spelman in 1864 and had 4 daughters and 1 son. He taught Sunday school and religiously gave 10% tithe to Erie Street Baptist Missionary Church. He was known to abstain from tobacco and alcohol.

John Rockefeller's Influences to Standard Oil

For 27 years, John Rockefeller was at the helm of Standard Oil. He started the company with Jabez Bostwick, Stephen Hardness, Samuel Andrews, Henry Flagler, and his brother William. The company was based in Ohio. He was known to some as the "robber baron" because the oil company had monopoly of oil refining in the US. He bought every component required for the manufacture of oil barrels so competitors weren't able to sell their product. Also, the price of Standard Oil was so low in order to undercut the competition.

Some competitors went out of business because they couldn't compete with the price of Standard Oil.

The Life of John Rockefeller after Retirement

When John Rockefeller retired, he spent his life in philanthropy. Although he had amassed great wealth, he also knew how to give to charity. He established the Rockefeller University and the University of Chicago. He also donated heavily to Spelman College, an African-American institution. He funded science, education, and medical research initiatives. His huge donations had helped eliminate hook worms and yellow fever.

John Rockefeller established the Rockefeller Sanitary Commission and the Rockefeller Institute for Medical Research. In 1902, he also established the General Education Board which aimed to provide equal opportunities of learning for everyone. He wanted the Board to make improvements to the higher education system as well as support medical schools in the country. He also wanted to develop agricultural practices and African-American schools in rural areas.

John D. Rockefeller also established the Rockefeller Foundation in 1913 with a donation of $250 million in order for the foundation to support arts, medical training, and public health. He was believed to have donated at least $600 million to different charities. Had he been alive in 2008, Forbes estimated his net worth to be worth $663.4 billion.

Marketing Lessons from John D. Rockefeller

Strive for efficiency

Edwin Drake used to pump crude oil from the Pennsylvania ground in 1859. When oil was discovered, other people joined the craze. "Wildcat" was the term they used to refer to the process of discovering oil by putting drilling rigs around Pennsylvania. Some people found oil while most people came home empty-handed. This exploratory oil digging was very time consuming and expensive. Crude oil was often lost.

John Rockefeller didn't want to "wildcat" for oil. He put up an oil refining enterprise. He was able to create kerosene when he heated refined oil at a particular temperature.

This lesson from Rockefeller can be applied even in marketing. Marketers may spend a lot of time and money chasing for leads by joining trade shows which weren't even fit for the products and services being marketed. A great amount of money is spent on demand generation systems which were ineffective. By striving for efficiency, a lot of waste can be prevented. Through the use of marketing automation systems, marketers will be able to generate the most feasible marketing return of investment. By knowing which programs can generate the best return of investment, marketers are able to plan not only the budget but the resources as well.

Be consistent

John Rockefeller made sure every stage in the oil refining process is owned by his company. He made significant investments in each stage. All the best materials had been used. He also had manufacturing sites for hoop iron and oil barrel. He also built drying and timber facilities. Sulfuric acid which was used in the oil purification process even had its own manufacturing plant. His company also owned storage holding tanks, warehouses, and oil tanker vehicles. Oil waste products were also processed in its own plant.

John Rockefeller owned every stage in the process because he wanted to control production. Because of this, he was able to produce the highest quality of kerosene which was used by different industries. His products had to be consistent in quality. Thus, his company was eventually changed to "The Standard Oil Company".

Marketers can again learn from Rockefeller by ensuring consistency in standard through marketing automation. Companies, especially those small and medium scale ones, often set out to use marketing automation to the fullest. However, they end out using it for email campaigns only. Processes must be aligned so that what gets passed to the sales team are of a particular expectation level and standard. Leads passed to the sales team mustn't be wasted and may be recycled.

Be adaptable.

John Rockefeller never stopped improving his products. Everything in his company had been measured and well accounted for. He was successful because he was able to get the necessary feedback through reports and metrics. He would often search for new ways to improve his ROI in sales, transportation, manufacturing, and staffing.

Rockefeller built his own pipelines when the railroad operators teamed up together and demanded that he pay a higher transportation fee. Eventually, the pipelines became a huge success while the railroads were destroyed.

When electricity replaced oil lamps, there was no need for kerosene anymore. Some people thought it was the end of John Rockefeller but he proved them wrong. He switched his business to the gasoline mass production.

Marketers can learn from this trait of John Rockefeller. They can continuously search for ways to improve. In the time of Rockefeller, reports and metrics proved to be a reliable backbone of his success. For marketers, available data can be used to adjust revenue stages when needed. The prospects' behavior must be monitored and the sales team must provide the feedback. The revenue cycle must be adapted at least 4 times a year so that the whole marketing to sales flow can be managed. The role of the marketer is to make sure that quality is standardized in the whole cycle.

The Legacy of John D. Rockefeller

Although his career as an oil refiner may be controversial, John Rockefeller made up for it through his philanthropic endeavors. Most of his competitors had been ruined while some competitors sold their businesses to Rockefeller. There were also some competitors who became wealthy because they worked with Rockefeller in his company.

However, a lot of people today know John Rockefeller because of his enormous wealth. In 1902, auditors reported that he was worth around $200 million. His wealth soared parallel to the demand for gasoline. His net worth was believed to be worth $900 million at the onset of World War I. When he retired, the New York Times estimated his net worth to be about $1.5 billion. When he died, he left about $1.4 billion in family trusts. According to some experts, if the basis of wealth calculation is on the ratio to the GDP, not even Sam Watson or Bill Gates can equal John Rockefeller's wealth.

His trusts and foundations continue to fund even political aspirations of his family. His grandson David Rockefeller became CEO of Chase Manhattan for 20 years. His other grandson Nelson Rockefeller became New York governor and 41st US Vice President. Another grandson, Winthrop Rockefeller became Arkansas governor while great grandson Jay Rockefeller was West Virginia governor and Senator. Another grandson, Winthrop Paul Rockefeller served as Arkansas Lieutenant Governor for 10 years.

The life of John D. Rockefeller is a typical rags-to-riches story. He was born to poor parents but it never became a hindrance to his success. He worked hard and continuously searched for ways to innovate. However, he never forgot where he came from. From his earnings, he was known to be a generous giver. He funded a lot of his philanthropic activities and strived to make a difference in the lives of other people. He was known to be the wealthiest person who had ever lived but much is also known for his big heart in helping others.

REID HOFFMAN

How He Got To Where He Is Now

These days, every person knows who Reid Hoffman is but only a few people know his story. He's been investing in a lot of start-up Silicon Valley companies. He was known to be Facebook's angel investor and Greylock Ventures' partner. He had investments in Airbnb, a home-sharing startup. However, Reid Hoffman is more popularly known as LinkedIn's Chairman and co-founder.

Reid Hoffman's fortune has grown to $2.3 billion primarily because share prices of LinkedIn have at least doubled within a year. He is known to own around 14.6% of the California-based professional social network company. Today, Hoffman spends time with LinkedIn and Greylock.

In 2004, Reid Hoffman shelled out $40,000 to Facebook. He was also known to have invested in Zynga, an online gaming company, when it was just starting. He is currently in various boards of nonprofit organizations especially Kiva, a not-for-profit organization which offers microfinancing. Hoffman was also part of "Paypal Mafia" before it was sold to eBay.

Prior to his stint at Paypal, Reid Hoffman founded SocialNet, a failed online dating site. In April 1998, together with Mark Zuckerberg and other Silicon Valley bigwigs, Hoffman supported FWD.US, a political group advocating reform in immigration.

Lessons from Reid Hoffman

Because a lot of people want to be entrepreneurs due to the developments in both technology and globalization, Ben Casnocha and Reid Hoffman co-authored "The Start-Up of You: Adapt to the Future, Invest in Yourself, and Transform Your Career". They recently shared tips on how to be successful in business even in these trying times.

First, each aspiring entrepreneur must search for the intersection of market realities, and his aspirations and strengths. Most experts suggest that he must use his strengths, know what the market needs, and follow his passions. But, according to Casnocha, each of the 3 can't be isolated from each other. He said a budding entrepreneur must know the intersection of the 3 and use it in his business plan.

The business plan will serve as a map for the first few years but it should be dynamic in nature. This means that the entrepreneur must be ready to adapt if there are challenges which had not been taken into consideration when the business plan was crafted. Because in reality, the market is ever changing, the entrepreneur's strengths will improve, and the passions will definitely change.

Second, a would-be entrepreneur must network. He must have a lot of acquaintances but a few allies. A budding entrepreneur must connect with professional and social networks in order to gain acquaintances in various professions and geographies because these people can be a source of diverse yet important information. According to Hoffman, it is also important for an entrepreneur to build a small network of collaborative yet emotionally rich relationships. He said that he and Mark Pincus, the founder of Zynga, knew how they will help one another. They agreed to be allies.

Lastly, an aspiring entrepreneur must learn when to take the risks. According to Canoscha, it isn't right to think of entrepreneurs as "crazy risk takers". He added that the entrepreneur must know when he can take risks especially when he had little information or when times are uncertain.

Risks should be assessed because the possible outcome may be devastating. The budding entrepreneur must think of the worst possible result and think if he and his business can survive it. If the answer is no then he may reconsider taking the risk.

Early Life of Reid Hoffman

Reid Hoffman went to Putney School in Vermont when he was in high school although he considered Berkeley as his childhood home. He went to Stanford when he was in college to major in symbolic systems, which is actually a combination of cognitive science and artificial intelligence. This course became the turning point in Hoffman's life because it got him interested in technology. He understood people because the course led to his understanding of the way people communicate and structure their thoughts.

He also went to Oxford University on a philosophy scholarship but he stopped after a year because he was just simply not interested with academics. What he did was approach venture capitalists and offered them some business ideas. However, he was asked to return to them if he had already shipped a product.

In 1993, he worked at Apple and later moved to Fujitsu. He came up with a list he needed before he can start his own company. He needed experiences in design, product management, product shipment, and building a team.

How Reid Hoffman Started His First Business

He started SocialNet, a site focused on online dating or on matching different kinds people who are seeking a certain kind of relationship. A person may be looking for a tennis partner, a roommate, a date, or a golf partner. He quit his Fujitsu job in July 1997 and started his own company. SocialNet partnered with various newspapers and magazines in order to draw people to the site. The strategy didn't work. Members of the board had differences in opinion and it was too difficult to resolve the issues so Hoffman left.

Reid Hoffman's Stint at Paypal

Reid Hoffman joined Paypal in November 1999. He brought up the idea of establishing another startup with Paypal CEO and co-founder Peter Thiel. Because Hoffman had been a member of Paypal's board since it began, Thiel told him to work with the company instead. Hoffman became head of external relations: international, banking, and corporate development.

How Reid Hoffman Started LinkedIn

When Paypal was sold to eBay, Hoffman and friends began thinking of other business ideas. In 2002, he formed a team and formed LinkedIn. Today, LinkedIn has at least 38 million users and a new member joins the site every second. They hired a lot of people in

2008 but had to cut the staff by 9% at the end of the year because the organization had to be rebalanced.

He hired Dipchand Nishar to handle operations so that he can concentrate on being CEO. Hoffman was interested in working through problems.

Reid Hoffman on Teaching How To Code

Recently, Bill Gates and Mark Zuckerberg supported Code.org's new initiative to encourage broader education in the field of computer science. General Assembly, an education startup, introduced a system for self-taught coding. Nancy Pelosi, House Minority Leader and Square CEO Jack Dorsey met to discuss a coding camp for girls.

Reid Hoffman is supporting the initiative because of 2 reasons: every employee must be able to build tech solutions and there is a need for more social good tech. According to him, even though not everyone can be hired for programming jobs, skills in coding are important. He believes that more cool solutions can be introduced if there are more people who know how to code. People who know basic coding can create prototypes which will make for a more innovative society.

Reid Hoffman also believes that if more people know how to code, more solutions can be developed for the common good. Some people may develop tutorial software which will reach more students across the world. Some individuals may be able to invent more things when they know how to code.

Teenager Brittany Wenger was able to develop a low-cost method to greatly improve the rate of cancer detection through the use of databases and artificial intelligence. According to Wenger, she was introduced to artificial intelligence and she became interested. She bought a programming book and taught herself how to code. If people aren't exposed to technology, nothing will be developed for the common good.

Furthermore, Reid Hoffman is a staunch supporter of upending the college diploma. He said higher education can be more effective and affordable if certification is overhauled. He is suggesting the use of new technologies on the diploma. The static piece of document can be made updateable, more connected, and richer if it includes a person's record of experience, expertise, and skills.

He is proposing an online profile like that of LinkedIn to replace the traditional diploma. Recently, LinkedIn made a move to invite school kids, as young as 14 years old, to join LinkedIn and create a professional profile.

Recently, Mozilla started offering Open Badges which allow users to receive badges for every skill they gained either online or offline. The badges can then be shared through social networks and other sites. According to Reid Hoffman, revolutionizing the way to earn the diploma can be a way to adapt to new technologies.

Reid Hoffman is now one of the richest men in the world. He failed a couple of times. He experienced difficulties and hardships but these setbacks didn't prevent him from striving real hard to make it to the top. He set out to make a difference and was very successful in what he does. People may currently experience some roadblocks in their quest for success right now. They shouldn't give up on their goals. They should take inspiration from the life of Reid Hoffman.

CORDIA HARRINGTON

CEO and President of the Bun Company

The life of Cordia Harrington, the CEO and President of The Bun Company, is a perfect example of a rags-to-riches story. She was born to struggling parents who couldn't keep up with their bills. She came from the working class whose parents couldn't afford to buy her new clothes. Thus, she had to settle with hand-me-downs. She, together with her family, treated her monthly McDonald's visit as a huge big night out. She was poor but she was determined to succeed.

Cordia Harrington's Career in Real Estate

With her $587, she took the challenge to become a real estate agent. She had a sign made in plywood in a rented room which she made as her office. She spent life in Arkansas selling homes. However, her contractors weren't able to give her a steady supply of houses to sell so she put up her own construction business so that she can also guarantee the quality of the houses she intended to sell. As she busied herself constructing and selling houses, she longed for more quality time with her children.

Cordia Harrington and Her Partnership with McDonald's

She opened her first McDonald's restaurant in small-town Effingham, Illinois. Back then, the town only had about 10,000 residents. To drive traffic to her McDonald's franchise, she bought a Greyhound Bus franchise and put up a bus station near her store. The strategy brought about 88 buses daily and at least 120 buses daily during summer. In fact, sales in this franchise were among the top 40 sales of all McDonald's restaurants across the United States of America.

Cordia Harrington acquired 2 more McDonald's stores in the Midwest. She had to work real hard for her stores to succeed. She became part of McDonald's business development committee and was assigned to the bun committee. She traveled the world to visit bakeries. She learned about Russian flour and Guatemalan sesame seeds.

Her imaginative and winning spirit led her to offer producing buns for the fast-food chain. She believed she can produce buns more efficiently. She was able to convince McDonald's honchos to give her buns a try.

At present, Cordia Harrington supplies English muffins and buns to McDonald's stores all around the world. She has partnered with other famous food distributors as well. She is affectionately called as "The Bun Lady".

Being CEO of "The Bun Company", Cordia Harrington manages 3 bakeries capable of producing at least 1,000 buns per minute for Pepperidge Farms and McDonald's. She also owns Bun Lady Trucking to ensure that her products arrive to the stores on time.

The Accolades Received By Cordia Harrington

In 2007, Cordia Harrington gave then-President George W. Bush a tour of her bakery. She was congratulated by the President for her success. She was named "Top 25 Women Business Builders" by Fast Company. She was inducted to the Nashville Board of the Federal Reserve Bank as well as to the Minnie Pearl Cancer Foundation Board. She helps support at least 18 Ronald McDonald Houses around the United States of America and China's Bethel Orphanage.

Lessons From Cordia Harrington

In an interview with Reader's Digest, Cordia Harrington said she got a lot of encouragement and love at home when she was just little. Her father would always tell her "You can do that!" When she was 11, she earned $60 during the summer teaching nursery kids at their backyard for 25 cents/3 hours. She also said that entrepreneurs would always find efficient ways to do things.

She always asks questions, even stupid ones, because she wants to learn. She has the desire to know a lot of things so she isn't afraid to ask. She admitted she wasn't an expert but it makes her team consider what she has to say. She also keeps a high standard of quality. In her bakeries, they aim for 2% rejects even though the industry standard is 4%. If the employees maintain such high standards, they are rewarded $50.

For Cordia Harrington, integrity is important if one wants to be successful. One must be able to deliver what he says he can do. Even when faced with the darkest moments of one's life, he has to keep going. He has to keep himself motivated in order to survive. Disappointments and trials may come. It is important for a person to have a strong will to succeed.

In another interview, she said that although orders from regular clients declined because of the recession, her company was able to survive because there were new clients who made up for the loss of sales from the regular customers. Being a member of the Federal Reserve Board, she said she saw the indicators that the country will go into a recession so she and the other members of the board decided that they won't lay off any of their workers. They accepted orders from clients even with no profit at all so that their employees will continue to have work. The workers were very appreciative of their efforts to keep them so they, in turn, worked hard to keep the business afloat. The employees were also rewarded whenever growth targets were met.

Being a leader, Cordia Harrington believes her leadership style is consensus building. She hears what other people have to say before she makes a decision because she says that she's not an expert. She has to listen to brilliant people in her team and tries to understand them before a decision is made. She has had a lot of mistakes in the past but she really makes it a point to listen to other people's ideas first.

On being a good leader, she says she has to ensure that the business is right on track. There may come a time that difficulties and hardships maybe unbearable that business owners may decide to sell their business. She says she's thankful she has stayed on and kept her business alive even when it could have been much easier to let go of the company during the most trying times.

In terms of hiring people, she said she has to hire and keep people who are not only brilliant but with an understanding of what the company stands for. These people must be able to understand not only their superiors but all the other workers in the company as well. Respect must be accorded to everyone.

According to Ms. Harrington, it is always good to take risks but it also better to have a backup plan if something goes wrong in the process. Entrepreneurs must accept the fact that not every business deal will push through and not everything will work according to the plan so it's always better to prepare backup plans just in case. As a good entrepreneur, a person must know flexibility. He must be able to realize that changes must be done to make the business keep up with the times. He must remain focused on what he intends to do and hire brilliant people who share the same vision with him. The right discipline and training will keep the business growing. As such, it is best for the entrepreneur to be always on his toes searching for new opportunities.

Check out some of the other JD-Biz Publishing books

<u>Gardening Series on Amazon</u>

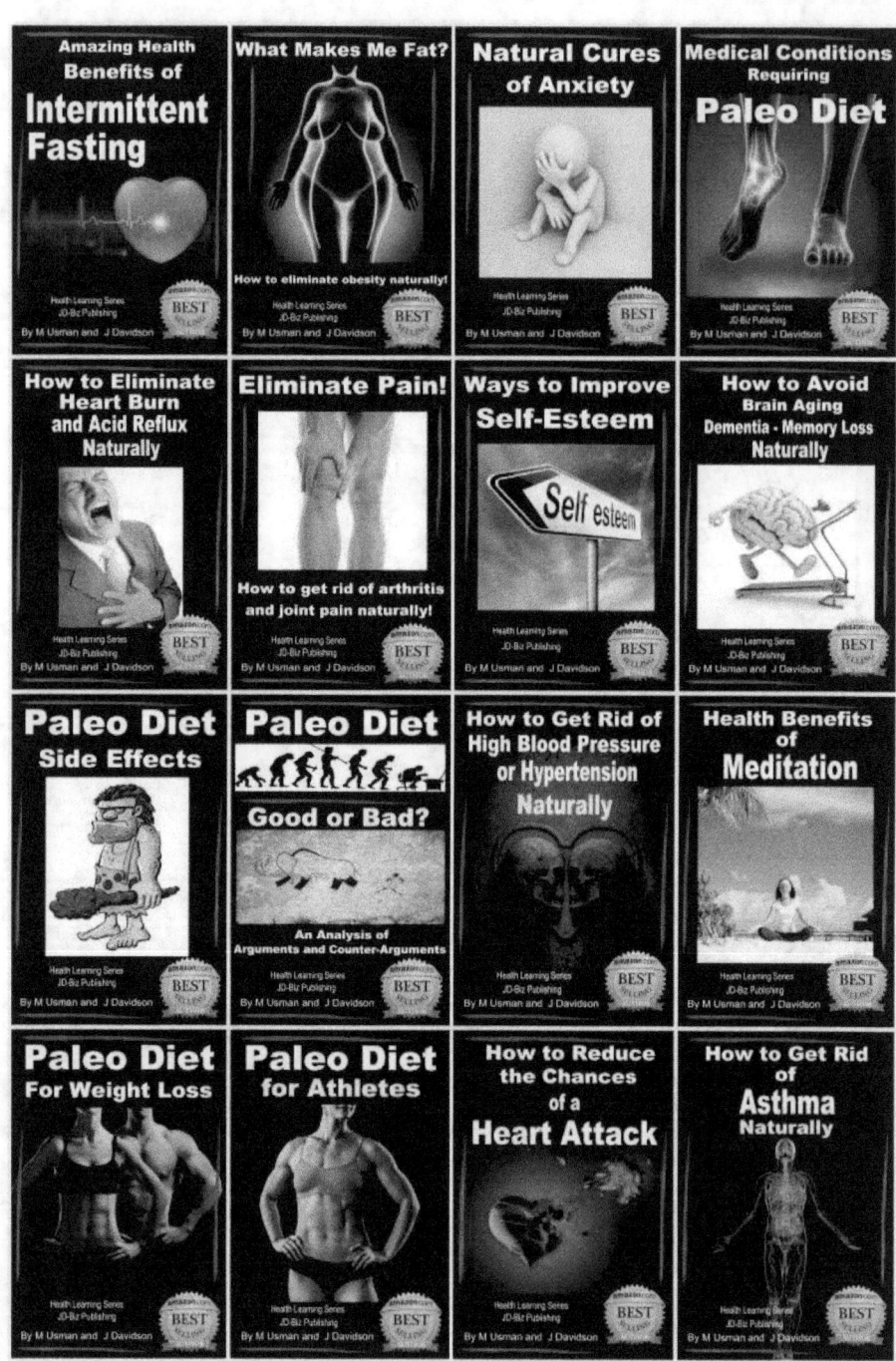

Amazing Health Benefits of **Intermittent Fasting**
Health Learning Series — JD-Biz Publishing — By M Usman and J Davidson

What Makes Me Fat?
How to eliminate obesity naturally!
Health Learning Series — JD-Biz Publishing — By M Usman and J Davidson

Natural Cures of Anxiety
Health Learning Series — JD-Biz Publishing — By M Usman and J Davidson

Medical Conditions Requiring **Paleo Diet**
Health Learning Series — JD-Biz Publishing — By M Usman and J Davidson

How to Eliminate **Heart Burn and Acid Reflux Naturally**
Health Learning Series — JD-Biz Publishing — By M Usman and J Davidson

Eliminate Pain!
How to get rid of arthritis and joint pain naturally!
Health Learning Series — JD-Biz Publishing — By M Usman and J Davidson

Ways to Improve **Self-Esteem**
Health Learning Series — JD-Biz Publishing — By M Usman and J Davidson

How to Avoid Brain Aging **Dementia - Memory Loss Naturally**
Health Learning Series — JD-Biz Publishing — By M Usman and J Davidson

Paleo Diet Side Effects
Health Learning Series — JD-Biz Publishing — By M Usman and J Davidson

Paleo Diet Good or Bad?
An Analysis of Arguments and Counter-Arguments
Health Learning Series — JD-Biz Publishing — By M Usman and J Davidson

How to Get Rid of High Blood Pressure or Hypertension **Naturally**
Health Learning Series — JD-Biz Publishing — By M Usman and J Davidson

Health Benefits of **Meditation**
Health Learning Series — JD-Biz Publishing — By M Usman and J Davidson

Paleo Diet For Weight Loss
Health Learning Series — JD-Biz Publishing — By M Usman and J Davidson

Paleo Diet for Athletes
Health Learning Series — JD-Biz Publishing — By M Usman and J Davidson

How to Reduce the Chances of a **Heart Attack**
Health Learning Series — JD-Biz Publishing — By M Usman and J Davidson

How to Get Rid of **Asthma** Naturally
Health Learning Series — JD-Biz Publishing — By M Usman and J Davidson

Amazing Animal Book Series

Learn To Draw Series

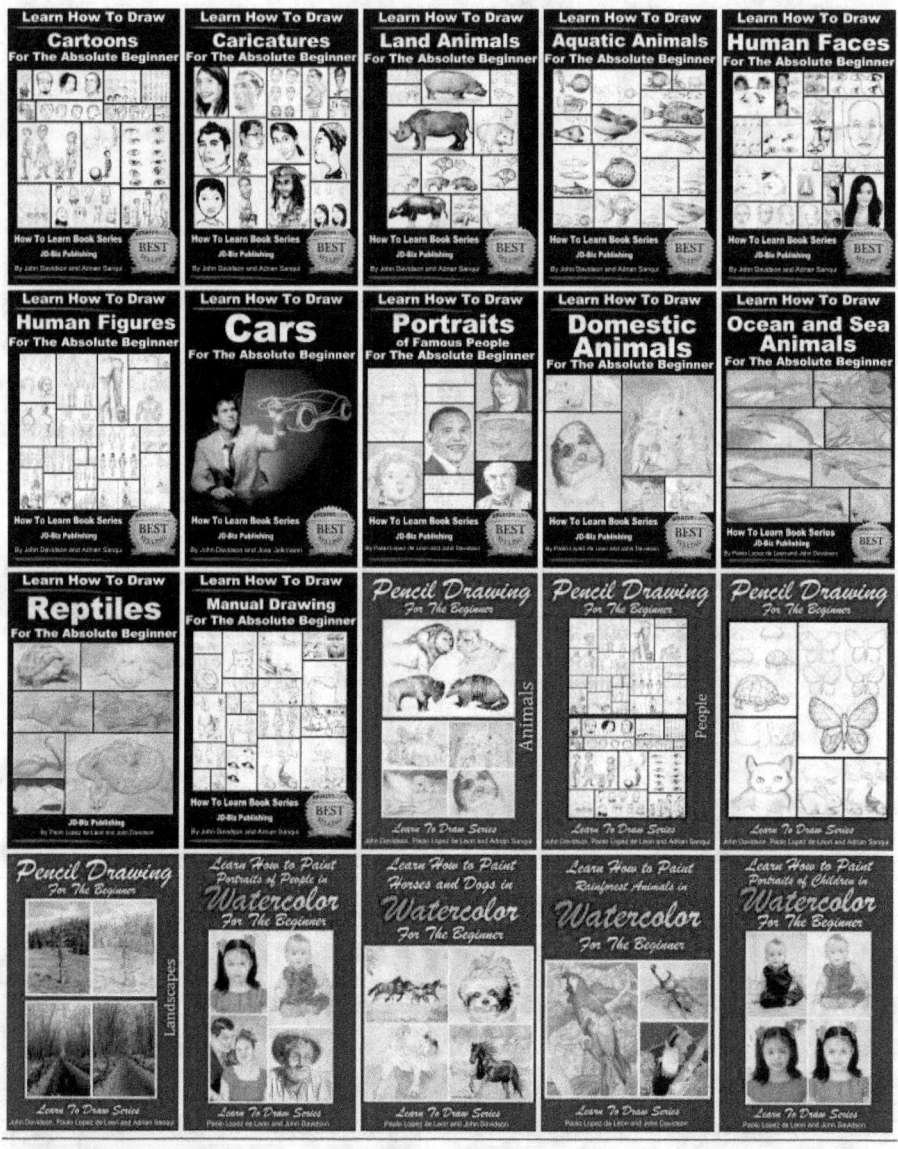

How to Build and Plan Books

Entrepreneur Book Series

Our books are available at

1. Amazon.com

2. Barnes and Noble

3. Itunes

4. Kobo

5. Smashwords

6. Google Play Books

Publisher

JD-Biz Corp

P O Box 374

Mendon, Utah 84325

http://www.jd-biz.com/